The Great Bicycle Experiment

The Army's Historic Black Bicycle Corps, 1896-97

Kay Moore

D0957706

2012
Mountain Press Publishing Company
Missoula, Montana

Cover photo: "Party of bicyclists climbing the terraces at Mammoth Hot Springs, Yellowstone National Park." Photographer F. Jay Haynes. Courtesy Haynes Foundation Collection, Montana Historical Society Research Center, Photograph Archives, Helena, MT.

Library of Congress Cataloging-in-Publication Data

Moore, Kay, 1950-
  The great bicycle experiment : the Army's historic Black Bicycle Corps, 1896-97 / by Kay Moore.
      p. cm.
  Includes bibliographical references and index.
  ISBN 978-0-87842-593-8 (pbk. : alk. paper)
  1. Military cycling—History—19th century. 2. United States. Army. Infantry Regiment, 25th. Bicycle Corps. 3. United States. Army—African American troops—History—19th century. 4. Fort Missoula (Mont.)—History—19th century. I. Title.
  UH33.M66 2012
  357'.52097309034--dc23

                                                2012021386

Printed in the United States

Mountain Press Publishing Company
PO Box 2399 • Missoula, MT 59806
(406) 728–1900
www.mountain-press.com

To all the men and women who protect this country through various types of service in the United States and abroad

and to the late

Dr. Armin Richard Schulz for his committed efforts to promote social justice through children's literature

Table of Contents

Preface

FIRST DISCOVERED THE STORY of the U.S. Army Bicycle Corps through an ad for the PBS video *The Bicycle Corps: America's Black Army on Wheels*. Immediately, I knew that this was a piece of American history that had to be shared with young people (and older people who don't know about it). Americans of all ethnicities can take pride in the little-known story of this group of courageous "Buffalo Soldiers" and their unique journey.

Learning to ride a bicycle is often viewed as a step toward personal independence. Metaphorically, the Bicycle Corps was a step toward personal independence for the African American soldiers who participated in the program. Although the key purpose of the Bicycle Corps experiment was never realized by the U.S. Army—bikes were never used in American military campaigns—the corps did achieve something important by showing the positive contribution African Americans could make to their country.

The history of the Bicycle Corps is a good example of how careful study of past events often reveals a deeper impact than was evident at the time. While doing research for this book, I found that the bulk of the source materials came from white participants and observers. Yet most documents showed positive attitudes toward the black soldiers—a bit surprising considering the racist mindset that was prevalent at the time. From this I concluded that the corps earned a measure of respect for their efforts and thus advanced, in a small way, the movement toward equality.

The African American soldier who participated in the Bicycle Corps certainly had experiences beyond the scope of the typical soldier of that era, white or black. While bicycle riding today is usually for pleasure or short-distance transportation, even riders of long-distance rides (like the Tour de France or cross-country fundraising treks) would not encounter the degree of difficulty endured by the corps. I was pleasantly surprised to find that some of what has been written about the Bicycle Corps was penned by bicycle enthusiasts as well as historians.

As is common in historical research, existing information often conflicts. I have done my best to sort out details and put the puzzle together in a way that presents the picture as accurately as possible. I hope you enjoy my efforts, and I encourage you to explore America's past for yourself.

"A new chapter in the history of liberty has been written. It has been shown that marching under the flag of freedom, animated by a love of liberty, even the slave becomes a man and a hero."
—Memoirs of Col. Thomas Morgan, 1885*

---

* From Lanning, Lt. Col. (Ret.) Michael Lee, *The African-American Soldier: From Crispus Attucks to Colin Powell* (New York: Citadel Press, 1999).

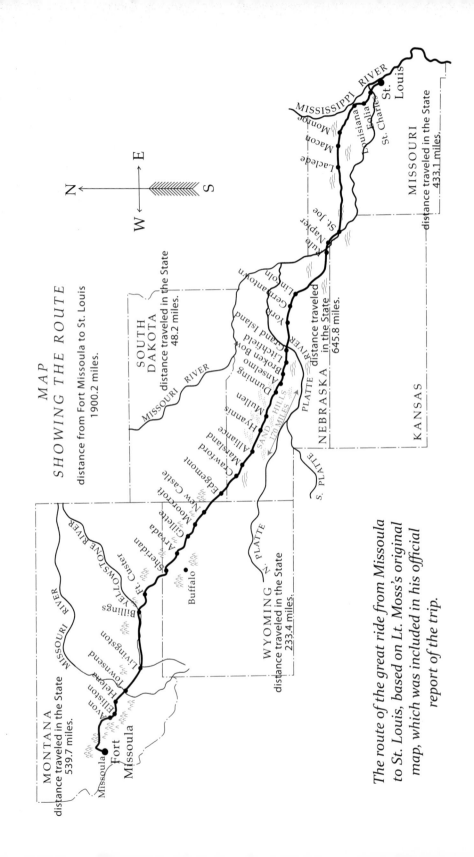

MAP
SHOWING THE ROUTE

distance from Fort Missoula to St. Louis
1900.2 miles.

MONTANA
distance traveled in the State
539.7 miles.

WYOMING
distance traveled in the State
233.4 miles.

SOUTH DAKOTA
distance traveled in the State
48.2 miles.

NEBRASKA
distance traveled
in the State
645.8 miles.

MISSOURI
distance traveled in the State
433.1 miles.

KANSAS

MISSOURI RIVER

YELLOWSTONE RIVER

MISSOURI RIVER

MISSISSIPPI RIVER

PLATTE RIVER

N. PLATTE

S. PLATTE

SAND HILLS.
170 MILES.

N
W   E
S

Missoula
Fort Missoula
Avon
Ellison
Helena
Townsend
Livingston
Billings
Ft. Custer
Sheridan
Buffalo
Arvada
Gillette
Moorcroft
New Castle
Edgemont
Crawford
Marsland
Alliance
Hyannis
Mullen
Dunning
Anselmo
Broken Bow
Litchfield
Grand Island
York
Germantown
Lincoln
Napier
St. Joe
Rulo
Macon
Laclede
Monroe
Bevia
Louisiana
St. Charles
St. Louis

The route of the great ride from Missoula
to St. Louis, based on Lt. Moss's original
map, which was included in his official
report of the trip.

1. The Buffalo Soldier

Pride and Prejudice

THERE HAS BEEN NO war fought by or within the United States in which African Americans did not participate, starting with the Revolutionary War (1776–83) and continuing to today. During the Civil War alone, there were twenty-five black Medal of Honor recipients. In his book *The African-American Soldier: From Crispus Attucks to Colin Powell* (1999), Lt. Col. (Ret.) Michael Lee Lanning notes: "For more than two hundred years, African Americans have participated in every conflict in United States history. They not only have fought bravely the common enemies of the United States but also have had to confront the individual and institutional racism of their countrymen."

In the Old West, soldiers were important players in the changes that occurred in the western United States in the late 1800s. Many of these were all-white regiments, but black soldiers did exist. Until World War II, American soldiers and sailors served in segregated units, and the U.S. Armed Forces were not fully integrated until the 1950s.

The first black military units on the western frontier were the 9th and 10th Cavalry Regiments, created by the United States

Congress on July 28, 1866. These were followed by the 24th and 25th Infantry Regiments. In those days, only whites could be commissioned officers, though there were some black noncommissioned officers, so these black units were commanded by whites.

Soldiers of the 25th Infantry train with Gatling gun in front of officers' quarters at Fort Missoula, late 1890s. Note that the officer (on the right, with a stripe on his pants leg) is white. —Courtesy Archives & Special Collections, Mansfield Library, University of Montana (84.332)

In addition to fighting Indians, who were resisting being forced off their homelands, black soldiers in the wild, wild West supported local law enforcement, protected railroads, escorted stagecoaches and wagon trains, and built roads and bridges. They also protected national parklands before the advent of federal park rangers.

The Native Americans who saw these servicemen called them "buffalo soldiers" because their dark curly hair reminded them of buffalo fur. The black soldiers knew that the nickname was a title of respect, as the buffalo was a revered animal to the Indians, and the 10th Cavalry featured the image of a buffalo on their emblem.

Unfair Treatment

ESPECIALLY IN THE EARLY DAYS, African American soldiers suffered much prejudice from their white counterparts and superiors. Some white officers refused to lead black regiments and even accepted a lower rank to be assigned to a white unit. An ad that appeared in the *Army and Navy Journal* on June 10, 1871, reflects this attitude: "A first Lieutenant of Infantry (white) . . . desires a transfer with an officer of the same grade, on equal terms if in a white regiment; but if in a colored regiment, a reasonable bonus would be expected."

Furthermore, black military units were often issued outdated weapons, old horses, poor quality clothing and food, and the worst housing. They frequently received the least desirable assignments with the lowest pay. "Negro" units were usually

Buffalo Soldiers of the 25ᵗʰ Infantry from Fort Keogh, Montana, at a winter camp near Glacier National Park, 1890. Note the mismatched clothing and gear. —Courtesy Library of Congress, Gladstone Collection

assigned to isolated posts, where contact with whites (military and civilian) was limited. When black soldiers encountered white troops in the field, conflicts sometimes erupted.

Under such conditions, you may well wonder why black men even enlisted in the military. Most African Americans were poor, and the army provided food, clothing, shelter, and $13 per month in salary. These basic things could be hard to acquire in civilian society, where opportunities for "colored" men were few. Furthermore, many believed what prominent African American leader Frederick Douglass had said to encourage black enlistment during the Civil War:

> "Once let the black man get upon his person the brass letters, U.S., let him get an eagle on his button, and a musket on his shoulder and bullets in his pocket, and there is no power on earth which can deny that he has earned the right to citizenship in the United States."

In spite of the difficulties, desertion rates in black units were lower and reenlistment rates were higher than in white regiments, as the Buffalo Soldiers fought to prove their worth. As we will see, they succeeded.

2. Fort Missoula, circa 1895

Life at a Frontier Army Post

LOCATED IN THE ROCKY MOUNTAINS, at the confluence of the Clark Fork and Bitterroot Rivers in western Montana, the town of Missoula was founded in 1864. At that time it was called Missoula Mills, for the flour mill and sawmill that had been built there, but "Mills" was soon dropped from the town's name. Settlement was sporadic at first. When Fort Missoula was built in 1877, there were about four hundred people living in Missoula. The town had a dirt main street, two general stores, and a few taverns.

The first railroad arrived in the area in 1883, attracting more settlers, and Missoula was incorporated as a city two years later. Lumber was a major industry. In 1893 the state's first university, the University of Montana, was established here. By the mid-1890s, when the Buffalo Soldiers were stationed at the fort, the city of Missoula had grown to nearly four thousand residents and had a full complement of hotels, restaurants, theaters, banks, shops, churches, professional services, and factories, as well as a streetcar line and even telephone service.

Street scene, downtown Missoula, 1894 —Courtesy Archives & Special Collections, Mansfield Library, University of Montana (82.0192)

The Fort

FORT MISSOULA RAISED ITS FLAG for the first time on November 8, 1877. Built to protect the fledgling community of Missoula from Indian raids, the fort had an open design with no stockade (defensive walls). Most of its nearly thirty buildings were oriented around a large parade ground. The soldiers who built the fort, two companies of the 7th U.S. Infantry, were white, as were the four companies of the 3rd Infantry, who replaced the 7th in November 1877.

Soldiers assigned to serve at Fort Missoula were lucky; many frontier posts were isolated, and the men stationed there had nowhere to go outside their fort for recreation, fresh food, or personal items. But the servicemen at Missoula were part of the community. Townspeople attended dances and concerts at the fort, and the soldiers spent much of their free time patronizing Missoula businesses (especially the taverns).

Long view of Fort Missoula, 1890s —Courtesy Archives & Special Collections, Mansfield Library, University of Montana (74.0160)

In 1888 Fort Missoula became home to the all-black 25th Infantry Regiment. For the most part, the people of Missoula were friendly toward the African American soldiers. There was generally less racial bigotry in the West than in the South, and throughout the 1800s, many black men and black families went west seeking greater opportunities.

The "negro" soldiers at Fort Missoula proved themselves to be competent and honorable soldiers who protected the townspeople and served the community very well. The editor of the *Anaconda* [Montana] *Standard* asserted that "They are model soldiers when in garrison, and their conduct whenever they have been called into the field has been excellent."

Daily Life at the Post

DURING ITS FIRST FEW YEARS at Fort Missoula, the 25th was sent out on a number of assignments to quell Indian disturbances, to guard trains, and to maintain order during labor disputes of area coal miners and railroad workers. Most of the soldiers' time, however, was spent doing routine tasks at the fort.

Life in the military was very structured. A soldier's day lasted from reveille (wake-up call) at 5:30 a.m. to lights out at 9:00 p.m.; these times varied slightly as the seasons changed. At Fort Missoula, a cannon was fired at reveille and at retreat (sundown) every day.

In between reveille and retreat, soldiers spent most of their time doing drills, chores, and guard duty according to a strict routine. The schedule was followed six days a week. On Sundays and some holidays, the soldiers had some free time, performing only the necessary duties, such as feeding the horses. The Fourth of July and Christmas were the two days each year that all soldiers got the day off.

In addition to participating in drills, marches, patrols, and shooting practice, some of the daily tasks soldiers performed at the fort included caring for the horses and mules; chopping and carrying wood for building, heating, and cooking; hauling water; constructing and repairing buildings at the fort; cleaning and repairing equipment such as firearms and saddles; and tending the post garden. Carrying out these physically demanding duties must have been uncomfortable most of the time, as the men had to wear heavy wool uniforms in both winter and summer.

The 25th Infantry performing field exercises near Fort Missoula, 1896 —Courtesy National Archives (111-SC-83772)

Those who shirked their duties or caused trouble could suffer harsh punishments. Military discipline was strict, and breaking rules could lead to confinement in the guardhouse, hard labor, a flogging, a stiff fine, or even a dishonorable discharge. One soldier caught taking a nap while on guard duty got six months in the guardhouse.

Soldiers of the 25th Infantry with mules and wagons near Fort Missoula, late 1890s —Courtesy Archives & Special Collections, Mansfield Library, University of Montana (86.0136)

Soldiers' meals were also structured. The men had twenty minutes for their morning and midday meals and thirty minutes for supper. Mealtime may have been a welcome break from work, but the food was usually not the tastiest. The army did not like to spend money on provisions, so supplies of flour, rice, coffee, sugar, and bacon were not high quality. Although the regulations manual listed delicious-sounding foods like beef pot pie and hot biscuits with butter and syrup, in reality, the beef was tough, the flour was coarse, and the butter was often rancid. When possible, the soldiers planted vegetable gardens and went fishing and hunting for fresh meat.

After the Civil War, the army took on the role of educating black soldiers. Due to the racial inequities in American society in those days, most African Americans received no formal schooling. The army was one of the few places where black men could get a basic education. Every black regiment was assigned a chaplain who not only conducted religious services but also taught the soldiers to read, write, and do arithmetic.

Overall, the Buffalo Soldiers at Fort Missoula had a decent life. This may be one reason they managed their responsibilities so well. When Lt. James Moss announced that the regiment would be taking part in a new, experimental assignment, they were surprised but ready and willing to face the challenge.

3. Why Bicycles?

A Transportation Experiment

THE SECOND HALF of the nineteenth century saw rapid technological change in America and all over the world. Transportation advances included the steamboat, the locomotive, the cable car, and the electric trolley. Horses were still a major form of transportation, but they had drawbacks, since they were expensive to keep and made messes on the streets. However, outside the cities and beyond the navigable rivers and railroad routes, horses were still the only option. Then, in the late 1800s, along came the bicycle.

The forerunner of the modern bicycle was invented by Karl von Drais of Germany in 1817. It had a wooden frame with handlebars and two iron wheels, but it had no pedals—the rider simply pushed the vehicle along with his feet. Drais dubbed his invention the "running machine," also called the Draisine. Improvements on Drais's device were made throughout the 1800s; innovations included adding pedals, making the frame lighter and sturdier, strengthening the wheels with spokes, and using tires made of rubber.

In the late 1860s a design for a two-wheel vehicle with a wood frame and rubber tires was patented with the name "bicycle," the first use of that term. They were also known as "boneshakers." A popular model during the 1870s and early 1880s had a large front wheel with a smaller back wheel; this design was commonly known as a "penny-farthing." By 1890 a version of the bicycle as we know it today, driven by a chain and with tires the same size and filled with air, had been developed.

Man with a penny-farthing style bicycle, circa 1900.
—Courtesy State Archives of Florida

With these improvements, cycling caught on in the United States and became a craze that spread like wildfire. Even in an isolated frontier town like Missoula, bicycles were popular. An article in an April 1894 edition of the local newspaper, the *Daily*

Missoulian, asserted that a person without a bicycle was not keeping up with the times.

How did cycling go from recreational riding to potential military transportation? By 1890, bicycles had already been used successfully for military purposes in many European countries, including Italy, France, Germany, Switzerland, Spain, and England. But whether bikes would work for the U.S. Army remained to be seen.

Bikes in the Military

BY THE 1890S, some American army officers had started questioning whether horses were the best way to move troops around. The animals had a number of disadvantages: 1) they needed food and water, which had to be found on the route or purchased and carried; 2) they needed rest, meaning occasional delays; 3) horses could die or be killed, leaving a soldier without transportation; 4) they might make noise and alert the enemy; and 5) horses sometimes panicked during the noise of battle and bucked their riders or refused to obey the riders' commands. But what was the answer? The time was ripe to try something new.

Lt. James Moss, stationed at Fort Missoula, was an avid fan of the popular new style of vehicle called the bicycle. Moss had graduated from the U.S. Military Academy at West Point in 1894 as a 2nd lieutenant. Having finished last in his class, Moss was assigned an undesirable post—the 25th Infantry regiment in Montana. Because of his undistinguished school record, the young lieutenant was determined to do well in his post and make his mark.

Lt. James Moss, Class of 1894, United States Military Academy
—Courtesy USMA archives

Combining his cycling experience with his military knowledge, Moss decided to suggest an experiment to test whether bicycles could be used instead of horses to transport soldiers overland. In April of 1896, Moss drafted a formal proposal requesting approval of his idea for testing out an experimental bicycle corps. The post commander, Col. Andrew Burt, endorsed the request, and it was sent to army headquarters.

Luckily for Lt. Moss, his letter crossed the desk of Gen. Nelson A. Miles. A few years before, General Miles had watched a six-day bicycle race at Madison Square Garden in New York City, and he had come to believe that the bicycle had great potential for use in the army. He had predicted, "The bicycle will in the future prove to be a most valuable auxiliary in military operations." In fact, Miles was already known as the "patron of military cycling" when he received Moss's request, and so he was eager to take the lieutenant up on his offer to put the bicycle idea to the test.

Before Lt. Moss submitted his proposal, Col. Burt had surveyed the men at Fort Missoula, asking who had experience riding a bike. Dozens of them reported that they had. Yet when Moss announced his plan, some of the Buffalo Soldiers were probably skeptical. The army had always used horses, especially on the frontier. How could a bicycle, a new-fangled contraption meant for leisure recreation, be of use to the military? Would the experiment really work?

4. Getting It Together

Organizing and Training the Bicycle Corps

WHEN LT. MOSS presented his plan for establishing a unit of soldiers who traveled on bicycles, some of the Buffalo Soldiers at Fort Missoula may have been doubtful, but Pvt. John Findley was immediately interested. Before joining the army, Findley had worked at the Imperial Bicycle Works in Chicago. He not only knew how to ride a bike but also how to fix one. When the lieutenant called for volunteers, Findley stepped right up. He would prove to be an invaluable member of the Bicycle Corps, showing the other men how to maneuver, maintain, and repair their vehicles.

Although the army had approved the creation of the Bicycle Corps, it had provided no funding for the bicycles. Moss contacted the Spalding Bicycle Company, which agreed to lend the army a number of specially designed bikes in return for allowing the company to use the corps in its advertisements. In addition, if the experiment succeeded and the military decided to use bicycles on a regular basis, Spalding could sell the army hundreds or even thousands of bikes.

The original 25th Infantry Experimental Bicycle Corps was composed of eight enlisted men from Companies B, F, and H: Sgt. Dalbert P. Green, Cpl. John G. Williams, Pvt. John Findley, Pvt. Frank L. Johnson, Pvt. William Proctor, Pvt. William Haynes, Pvt. Elwood Forman, and musician William W. Brown. These soldiers would undergo the initial training and lay the groundwork for the corps' first major trip.

The 25th Infantry in formation at Fort Missoula, 1896 —Courtesy National Archives (111-SC-83771)

On July 11, 1896, an article appeared in the *Daily Missoulian* under the headline "Army on Wheels, Bicycle Corps, Organized by Lieutenant Moss of the Twenty-fifth Infantry":

Today is a red letter day for cycling in the United States army. The twenty-fifth Infantry Bicycle Corps has been organized at Fort Missoula, and is the first organization of the kind effected in the regular army. The object of the corps is to thoroughly test the practicability of the bicycle for military purposes in a mountainous country. The corps is to consist of eight picked men, commanded by Lieut. J. A. Moss, and as all of the men are very enthusiastic there is no doubt that great results will be accomplished.

Preparations Begin

THE EIGHT CHOSEN MEN spent the first part of the summer of 1896 training with the bicycles, riding fifteen to forty miles a day. The men had to learn many things, including how to ride without their hands and how to shoot a gun from a moving bicycle. The men also practiced carrying their bikes through deep water. To do this, they worked in pairs; hanging one bike and its load on a long wooden pole, each man held one end of the pole and crossed the water holding it above his head to keep the bike and equipment dry. Then they returned for the other man's bike and repeated the procedure.

Perhaps the hardest exercise was scaling a nine-foot fence. The eight soldiers lined up in front of the fence, dismounted their bikes, and leaned them up against the fence. On the command "Jump Fence!" six of the men climbed the fence by standing on the seats of their bikes and pulling themselves up; three of them jumped down to the other side while the other three stayed on top of the fence. The two men left with the bicycles each lifted a bike and hoisted it up to one of the men on top, who in turn handed it down to a man on the other side. This was repeated until all the bikes were moved. Finally the last two men scaled the fence, helped up by the men on top, then they all jumped down and remounted their bikes. They had to complete the whole routine within twenty seconds to satisfy Lt. Moss.

After three weeks of training, Lt. Moss decided that the men were ready for their first overnight trip.

The soldiers hold their bikes above their heads while crossing a stream in this undated photo. —Courtesy Archives & Special Collections, Mansfield Library, University of Montana (672.239)

5. Gearing Up

Trial Run to Lake McDonald

LIEUTENANT Moss decided to take only six men on the corps' first trial. He mapped out a 126-mile round-trip route to Lake McDonald, a beautiful lake in the Mission Mountains about fifty miles north of the fort as the crow flies. The expedition would involve four days of rigorous travel and three nights of camping.

In preparation for the journey, Moss made a list of provisions that included about 120 pounds of food, divided among the riders. The total food supply included 35 lbs. flour, 19 lbs. canned beans, 20 lbs. bacon, 2 lbs. salt, 5 lbs. prunes, 6 lbs. sugar, 5 lbs. rice, 5 lbs. canned corn, 2 lbs. coffee, and other items. These rations, along with cooking and eating utensils, extra clothes, personal-care items, and bicycle-repair parts and tools, went into various sacks and boxes that were strapped to the bike; bedrolls and tents were secured over the handlebars. Each soldier also carried a rifle and fifty rounds of ammunition.

This display at the History Museum at Fort Missoula shows the type of bicycle and gear used by the Bicycle Corps. None of the corps' original bikes exist, as they were all sent back to the Spalding Bicycle Company. —Photo by Jay Kettering

The First Adventure

THE SIX-MAN BICYCLE CORPS left Fort Missoula on the morning of August 6, 1896, bound for Lake McDonald. The weather had been rainy, and the dirt roads were mired with mud. The thick muck forced the men to stop often to wipe off their tires. It also made steep hills too slick to climb, so sometimes the riders had to dismount and walk. Even in drier areas, many of the roads were rocky and took extra effort to ride over. In some places, fallen trees blocked their way. At times the soldiers ended up walking their bicycles along the railroad tracks.

That night, the corps camped at Mission Creek. In spite of the obstacles, they had traveled over fifty miles that day. The next afternoon they reached Lake McDonald, its shining waters framed by the magnificent Mission Mountains. As Lt. Moss noted in his trip journal, the gorgeous scenery and excellent fishing made up for the difficulties of the ride: "From our camp we could plainly see on the mountain tops the snowbanks from which the lake was born. Its water abound with delicious trout and two or three of the soldiers who brought lines along caught them nearly as fast as they could pull them out."

For supper that night, along with the trout, the soldiers had biscuits, bacon, corn, prunes, and coffee. Despite their exhausting ride, the men found they weren't tired and stayed up until 11 p.m. talking and telling jokes while a steady rain beat against the sides of their tents.

Problems abounded as they started back to the fort the next day. The continuing rain drenched the men, and their wet,

Lake McDonald in the Mission Mountains of Montana, circa 1920
—Courtesy Archives & Special Collections, Mansfield Library, University of Montana
(741.009)

heavy uniforms made movement difficult. As they walked the bicycles, their shoes filled with slippery, sticky mud. The bikes, struggling through muddy, rocky, rut-filled roads, needed constant wiping, adjustments, and repairs. The men had to stop frequently to fix flat tires, broken foot pedals, and damaged chains. The crossing of one deep creek loosened the cement on the tires and caused them to fall off their wooden rims, so the expedition had to halt once again to glue them back on. Lt. Moss remarked that "had the devil himself conspired against us we would have had but little more to contend with."

The party finally reached Fort Missoula on August 9, having traveled 126 miles in four days. Although the trip had severely challenged both men and bicycles, Lt. Moss considered it a success. In fact, in a way, it was lucky that they had faced so many obstacles because it proved what the Bicycle Corps could accomplish in spite of rough roads and bad weather. Moss immediately began planning another, longer test run, and only six days later, the corps was off again.

6. The Second Trial

Expedition to Yellowstone

THE SECOND EXPERIMENT would take the corps to Yellowstone National Park, about 325 miles east of Fort Missoula by road and trail. Lt. Moss would take all eight riders on this three-and-a-half-week trek. Preparations were similar to those for the first trip, but a few new items were added, including some medical supplies and a lot of spare bicycle parts. Jelly, sausage, and chocolate were added to the food rations, and the men carried some extra clothes and personal items. To help document the trip, Lt. Moss took a Kodak camera and seven rolls of film along with a notebook.

Yellowstone National Park, most of which lies in Wyoming, was the world's first national park, created by Congress in 1872. Most Americans had heard about the amazing geysers and hot springs, and the soldiers of the Bicycle Corps were excited to have the opportunity to see them firsthand. They rode out of Fort Missoula on August 15, 1896.

Following the Lieutenant ●●●●●●

THE JOURNEY WOULD TAKE the riders across most of the state of Montana, through the mountain passes of the western side and over the vast plains of the eastern side. Along the way, they passed through many rural communities, where the townspeople were surprised to see a group of African American soldiers riding bicycles, with camping gear strapped to their handlebars and their heads held high. In virtually every town, the people were friendly to the men and often cheered them on. Sometimes the men stopped to trade or buy food items, such as milk and eggs, from the people they met, to supplement their rations.

The route to Yellowstone mostly followed the railroad lines, enabling Lt. Moss to arrange for supplies to be held for them at various train stations; this way, the men didn't have to carry as much stuff. A few times, however, the expedition got delayed and ran out of food before they got to the station. On one occasion, musician Brown got so hungry he ate some wild fruit that made him very sick. Lt. Moss put the ailing soldier on a train to meet the group at a later stop.

As the corps neared Yellowstone, they happened to meet the famous artist Frederic Remington, who was riding with another Buffalo Soldier unit, a cavalry corps from Fort Assiniboine. Later, in an article for *The Cosmopolitan Magazine* (February 1897), Remington mentioned the encounter: "After breakfast the march begins. A Bicycle Corps pulls out ahead. It is heavy wheeling and pretty bumpy on the grass, where they are compelled to ride, but they manage far better than one would anticipate."

Averaging about forty-five miles a day over uneven terrain, with one day of rest, the corps reached Fort Yellowstone in eight and a half days. The men spent the next week resting and touring the park. They picnicked, fished, and enjoyed the sights, including Old Faithful Geyser. Many of the park's tourists were curious about the corps and came over to ask them questions, look over their gear, and take pictures. Some of these photos still survive and are now regarded as historical treasures. When one person asked a soldier where they were going, he replied, "The Lord only knows. We're following the lieutenant."

The Bicycle Corps walking their bikes along a railroad track, date and place unknown. The soldiers often followed railroad tracks on their trip to Yellowstone and to St. Louis. —Courtesy Archives & Special Collections, Mansfield Library, University of Montana (672.240)

Bicycle Corps on Minerva Terrace in Yellowstone National Park
—Courtesy Haynes Foundation Collection, Montana Historical Society Research
Center Photograph Archives, Helena, MT (H-3614)

As they explored the park and its natural wonders, the Buffalo Soldiers "were delighted with the trip and in the best of spirits the whole time," Moss reported. Indeed, Moss describes several scenes where the men are having fun and cracking jokes. On August 27, the group passed a marker pointing the way to a geyser basin called West Thumb. The sign said "W. Thumb." One of the soldiers joked that he'd heard of crooked thumbs, sore thumbs, and broken thumbs, but he had never heard of a

"W" thumb. Later that day, the men reached the Continental Divide and decided to have some fun. Dividing into two groups, they stood on each side of the imaginary line and shook hands. One of the men on the eastern side quipped, "Well, old man, how's everything with you way down there on the Pacific slope?" Someone on the other side answered, "Oh, everything is fine with us! How's things getting along with you fellas way down there on the Atlantic slope?"

Bicycle Corps on terraces at Mammoth Hot Springs, Yellowstone National Park —Courtesy Haynes Foundation Collection, Montana Historical Society Research Center Photograph Archives, Helena, MT (H-3616)

Bicycle Corps crossing bridge in Yellowstone National Park
—Courtesy National Archives (111-SC-88518)

The corps started on their return trip on September 1. They ran into heavy rains on their first day out, causing difficulties and delays. The soldiers began to complain, though good-naturedly, one of them saying, "A mule! A mule! My kingdom for a mule!" while another quipped, "There were no bicycles one hundred years ago. Oh, how I wish I lived one hundred years ago!" Nevertheless, they covered fifty-eight miles before taking shelter for the night in a rancher's shed.

The next day, the roads were even worse. One bicycle was badly wrecked, but the soldiers met a traveling cyclist who fixed it. The third day was better, and in spite of the hot sun and another flat tire, the corps covered an amazing seventy-two miles. For the next several days, strong winds and bad roads slowed them down, but they pushed on, finally reaching their home fort at 7:45 p.m. on September 8. They had traveled a total of 790 miles on bicycles.

Once again, Moss was pleased with the outcome of his experiment. According to his notes, the soldiers had been "delighted with the trip—treated royally everywhere—thought the sights grand." The next trip would be the biggest challenge of all—a 1,900-mile journey halfway across the continent.

Bicycle Corps posing with their bikes in Yellowstone National Park
—Courtesy National Archives (111-SC-88516)

7. The Big Idea
Two Thousand Miles on Two Wheels

LIEUTENANT MOSS THOUGHT the corps' successful trip to Yellowstone had proven the usefulness of bicycles to the army, but the top military men were not convinced. Moss believed that another expedition would sway them if it covered more distance over more varied terrain and through any type of weather and road conditions. He got to work planning a route that would meet these requirements.

The corps, Moss decided, would ride from Missoula to St. Louis, Missouri, a journey of almost 2,000 miles across a large portion of the United States. He chose this route because it would pass through "high and low altitudes; moist and dry climates; up grades and down grades; the mountainous and stony roads of Montana; the hummock earth roads of South Dakota; the sandy roads of Nebraska and the clay roads of Missouri."

The plan was to leave Fort Missoula on June 14, 1897. The route would roughly follow the Northern Pacific Railroad line through Montana, from Missoula to Billings, then trace the Burlington Northern Railroad from Wyoming to Nebraska. From there, the corps would follow the Missouri River to St. Louis.

The unit's motto, "Onward," as shown on their emblem, seemed especially appropriate for this mission.

Even though being in the Bicycle Corps was physically demanding and life on the trail was challenging, forty soldiers volunteered for the trip. Lt. Moss selected twenty men, ranging in age from twenty-four to thirty-nine, all in top physical condition. Army regulations stated that cyclists must weigh no more than 140 pounds and be no taller than five feet, eight inches. But some of Moss's chosen men were outside this range, so Lt. Moss got special permission to include them.

Only five soldiers in the new group—Haynes, Frank Johnson, Proctor, Forman, and Findley—had taken part in the previous year's trips. One man didn't even know how to ride a bicycle yet. The final list of twenty included men from Companies B, F, G, and H:

Sgt. Mingo Sanders	*Pvt. William Proctor*
Lance Cpl. William Haynes	*Pvt. Elwood Forman*
Lance Cpl. Abram Martin	*Pvt. Richard Rout*
Musician Elias Johnson	*Pvt. Eugene Jones*
Pvt. John Findley	*Pvt. Sam Johnson*
Pvt. George Scott	*Pvt. William Williamson*
Pvt. Hiram L. B. Dingman	*Pvt. Sam Williamson*
Pvt. Travis Bridges	*Pvt. John Wilson*
Pvt. John Cook	*Pvt. Samuel Reid*
Pvt. Frank L. Johnson	*Pvt. Francis Button*

The corps was divided into two squads, with Cpls. Haynes and Martin as leaders. Because it would be such a long and hazardous trip, one of the fort's physicians, Dr. James M. Kennedy, was also asked to join the party. In addition, a young newspaper reporter from the *Daily Missoulian*, Edward Boos, went along to track the expedition's progress and send reports to the paper. Pvt. Finley again served as the corps' mechanic, the main person responsible for keeping the bicycles working. His bicycle was heavier than the others and was fitted with a metal toolbox.

Journalist Edward H. Boos, who accompanied the Bicycle Corps to St. Louis and reported on the trip. This photo is undated, but Boos appears to be young, so it may have been taken near the time of the Bicycle Corps. Boos was only nineteen when he accompanied the soldiers in 1897. —Courtesy Archives & Special Collections, Mansfield Library, University of Montana (78.0162)

Getting Ready for the Long Haul

SINCE RETURNING FROM YELLOWSTONE, the men of the Bicycle Corps had continued their training, running several practice maneuvers and trying various operations before the cold weather set in. Lt. Moss spent most of the winter preparing for the St. Louis expedition. His plans included a detailed schedule and meticulous lists of gear and provisions.

After the Bicycle Corps' Yellowstone trip, Moss penned a brief account of the adventure called "Military Cycling in the Rocky Mountains," published in February 1897 by the Spalding Bicycle Company. Moss's image and words also appeared in a few ads for Spalding. In exchange, the company lent Moss the bicycles for the cross-country trip.

The bicycles, which arrived on June 4, 1897, were built to the most modern design of the time, with steel frames and rims. While this made them heavy and bulky, it was hoped that they would be sturdier and that the cement for the tires would adhere better to the steel frames than it had to the wooden ones. The bicycle chains were covered with rubber casing for protection, and an improved seat design would increase comfort. The corps would test out eight different brands of tires along the way.

The food provisions for this trip were more basic than the ones taken on the earlier trips. The rations included bacon (cut into small chunks and wrapped in cloth), flour, baking powder, salt, pepper, canned beef, canned beans, coffee, and sugar. Resupply stops were about 50 to 120 miles apart, or one to two days' riding. The list of repair tools and spare parts, however,

Lt. Moss's 1897 booklet "Military Cycling in the Rocky Mountains" was based on his experiences with the Bicycle Corps in 1896. The Spalding Bicycle Company published it to promote their bikes.

was much more extensive than the one for the shorter trips—the men carried hundreds of items for this purpose.

As before, each man would again carry a blanket roll strapped to his handlebars. The bundle included gear for shelter and sleeping, extra clothing, and some personal items (soap, towel, toothbrush and toothpowder, etc.) for a total weight of about ten pounds. In addition, each man carried enough food for two days and eating utensils, stored in a hard leather case that was attached to the bike frame. Cooking utensils were carried in metal cases strapped under the handlebars. When all the gear was loaded on the bicycle, it weighed about 59 pounds, plus a ten-pound rifle and fifty rounds of ammunition in a cartridge belt. Adding the weight of the soldier himself (an average of 148 pounds), each bike carried about 220 pounds.

The corps was loaded and ready to roll at 5:30 a.m. on June 14, 1897. That day, the *Daily Missoulian* ran this headline: "Off for St. Louis: Twenty-fifth Infantry Bi-Cycle Corps Takes Up Its Long March." The article called it "one of the most important journeys ever taken out of Missoula."

The Bicycle Corps pedaling out of Fort Missoula on their way to St. Louis, June 1897 —Courtesy Archives & Special Collections, Mansfield Library, University of Montana (80.0047)

8. And They're Off!

St. Louis or Bust

LTHOUGH THE CORPS left Fort Missoula in the early morning of June 14, 1897, quietly and without fanfare, once the men reached town, they found local residents lined up along the road to cheer them on. The soldiers appreciated this gesture, and to give the folks a little show, Moss had the cyclists ride through town in an impressive double-line formation.

Mother Nature, however, was not so kind to the Bicycle Corps. On the first afternoon, a rainstorm rapidly turned the dirt roads into sticky mud, and the men had to ride through weeds and underbrush to avoid the muck of the roadbed. Even under these trying conditions, the soldiers traveled fifty-four miles that day. At about 8:00 p.m., they pitched their camp at Cottonwood, Montana (near today's Clearwater Junction).

On the first night, the heavy rains returned, and in the morning the roads were impassable. To reach the first supply point, however, the soldiers had to ride more than fifty miles that day or go hungry. Fighting rain and wind, the men had to dismount and walk their bicycles many times that day. Nevertheless, they made it to their destination, Avon, Montana, around eight o'clock that night, having traveled fifty-eight miles.

MILITARY PURPOSES.

Bicycle Trip by Soldiers to Determine if the Wheel is Available as a Transport.

ITS PRACTICABILITY IS TO BE TESTED.

Why Lieutenant Moss and Command of the United States Army are on Their Journey.

The bicycle corps of the Twenty-fifth Infantry, U. S. A., which left Missoula Monday morning, June 14th, for St. Louis, Missouri, is now between Helena and Bozeman, and as the weather has improved will make better time than was made between Missoula and Helena, owing to the muddy condition of the roads. Why the trip was undertaken is fully explained in what follows:

Not many years ago the bicycle was looked upon as a mere toy, a kind of "dandy horse," and the riders were regarded as fit subjects for pity. That time, however, is a thing of the past; the bicycle of today is a very important factor in our social and commercial life, and bids fair to figure conspicuously in the warfare of the future. France, Austria, Switzerland, England, Germany and other European powers, have, of late years, devoted considerable attention to the bicycle as a machine for military purposes, resulting in its adoption as component parts of their armies.

ate of her health was much helped. My ife kept on using the pills and likewise ept getting better. In a comparatively short me her condition was more healthy than for

When setting up camp, the men took turns doing the necessary tasks, such as collecting wood, building fires, and cooking. Sometimes a small group would go out to fish or hunt to supplement their rations. As was typical in the army in those days, the corps members slept two men to a tent. Each soldier carried half of a tent and half of the tent poles on his bike, and the shelters were assembled in teams of two. The tents were so small that one soldier joked that "you crawled in your tent and stayed crawled until you were ready to get out."

As the journey wore on, the expedition continued to struggle through bad weather and rough road conditions, and mosquitoes plagued them almost daily. Sometimes when the roads

The corps in camp somewhere en route to St. Louis in 1897 —Courtesy Archives & Special Collections, Mansfield Library, University of Montana (73.0030)

were very muddy, the soldiers tried pedaling over the railroad tracks, which, as reporter Boos described it, "nearly jolted [us] to pieces." If they encountered a sizable stream, the men had to carry their heavily loaded bicycles across on their shoulders. On steep hills, several riders had to contend with runaway bicycles zooming out of control.

As they approached the Continental Divide, the corps was greeted with blowing snow and freezing temperatures. No celebration this time! Getting down to lower elevations, they had to cross ankle-deep water created by the melting snow.

A crowd gathered around the corps in an unknown town along the route, 1897 —Courtesy Archives & Special Collections, Mansfield Library, University of Montana (672.271)

In spite of the hardships, the journey had its interesting moments. Many of the people the corps met along the way were curious about these bicycle-riding Buffalo Soldiers. Some townsfolk had never seen black skin before. Lt. Moss stated, "The Corps attracted a great deal of attention as we rode through these rural mountain districts. Horses and cows ran from us, and the inhabitants would stop their work and gaze at us in astonishment." While they may have been puzzled at first, the local people were usually friendly and helpful, often giving the soldiers meals and places to stay. In a tavern in Big Timber, Montana, one old Civil War veteran bought drinks for the entire company. Another time, an elderly German couple gave them milk, bread, and cakes.

Fort Custer and a Solemn Anniversary

THE BICYCLE CORPS REACHED Billings, Montana, on day ten. Here they stopped for some supplies and rested a few hours before heading on toward Fort Custer. The road was so muddy that they did not make it very far—about thirteen miles in three hours. They camped near Pryor Creek, on the Crow Indian reservation, spending the night at an abandoned Indian lodge they found.

By this time, the expedition's rations had nearly run out, and the next morning, a piece of burnt toast and a cup of coffee were all the men had for breakfast. This was their last meal until they reached the next supply point, Fort Custer, at 10:30 that night. Moss wrote that it was "one of the hardest days we ever had."

The next day, the corps rested a while at the comfortable fort, then rode the short distance to the Little Bighorn Battlefield to see the place where Gen. George Custer and his 7th Cavalry had met their end. It was an emotional moment—the men arrived at the battlefield on June 25, 1897, the twenty-first anniversary of the fateful fight. The soldiers of the Bicycle Corps fell silent when they beheld the somber scene—dozens of small white tombstones, which marked the cavalrymen's graves, lay scattered across the field, along with the sun-bleached bones of some of their horses. The Buffalo Soldiers felt deeply the importance of their journey that day. They camped near the wooden cross on which was written "Here fell Custer."

Modern photo of graves at Little Bighorn Battlefield National Monument. —Courtesy Bill and Jan Moeller

A Hard Road through the Middle

AFTER DEPARTING FORT CUSTER on June 26, the corps passed a barbed-wire fence that marked the Montana-Wyoming border. At first the weather was better, but late in the day the men were caught in another rainstorm. Reaching Parkman, Wyoming, they found an old barn to spend the night in.

In spite of all the rain, drinking water became hard to find as the men traversed Wyoming, South Dakota, and Nebraska. Many of the streams and pools they found contained water that was too alkaline to drink. Anyone who swallowed this salty-tasting water would likely become sick.

In the meantime, the roads had not improved—in some places they were even worse than before. Every day put the men into a deeper exhaustion. Already behind schedule, the corps suffered further delays due to bad weather, poor roads, bike damage, and minor illnesses.

One evening, on their way to Moorcroft, Wyoming, Moss decided to push on through the night to their destination. He described the episode in his journal: "Feeling our way along a road, wet and muddy from a rain from the previous day, we walked and walked and walked, pushing our wheels before us." They stumbled through the darkness for hours. At one point, Moss heard a strained voice whisper, "My God . . . I can't go any further." The men finally collapsed on the ground around 2:00 a.m. When they awoke a few hours later, they saw the red buildings of Moorcroft in the early morning light, only about a mile away.

RECEIVED A WELCOME.

Twenty-fifth Infantry Bicycle Corps at Crawford, Nebraska on the Fourth.

A REST OF HALF A DAY AT MARSLAND.

Through Sand and Over Railroad Track Land of Rattlesnakes and Jack Rabbits.

Whitman, Nebraska, July —.The Fourth of July celebration was at its height when the 25th U. S. Infantry Bicycle corps arrived at Crawford. The town was full of people and the corps was given a hearty welcome. A number of soldiers from Fort Robinson, four miles distant, were in town and took the men in charge while in their midst.

One day's rations were received at Crawford and distributed among the men. At 5 o'clock assembly was sounded and in a few minutes the corps left the town, passing through the big crowds on the main street amid loud cheers. The run for the evening was for Belmont, which was reached about 8 o'clock. Camp for the night was made in a farmer's yard, who kindly furnished hay for bedding and wood for fuel.

Six o'clock on the morning of July 4th found us on the road to Marsland, which was reached in an hour's run; here a stop was made of over a half a day in honor of the nation's birthday. Before leaving, rations for two days were received and distributed.

From Marsland to Alliance a great variety of roads was encountered, sandy, steep hills, rough and untraveled, and a stretch of 20 miles of the best road we had yet traveled over. The route lay across a meadow leaving Marsland and across a large hill to a table land where the road was nearly level. We reached Hemingford at 4 o'clock and stopped a half hour. Leaving the latter place, a surprise awaited us—an actually good road, better than promised, and almost level. The corps was pleased and made an effort to break all previous records; everyone flew. At the end of the first 35 minutes nine miles were behind us, and at 6 o'clock the entire corps was at Alliance on their camping grounds, having covered 20 miles at a rate of four and a half minutes for each.

An extra good supper was prepared. Lieut. Moss purchased a quantity of fresh meat, baker's bread and a stock of groceries, and by 8 o'clock the men had their grand Fourth of July spread, eating the same in the presence of the entire town which had turned out to see the corps.

On July 5th the thoughts of sand hill terrors and tortures were upon the minds of every member of the corps as we pedaled away from Alliance at 4:30 that morning. It was but a run of six mile on a good road before we were in the midst of what had been our dread ever since leaving home, the sand hills of Nebraska. The road suddenly changed from a hard smooth path to a soft shifting mass of sand.

After passing through the southwestern corner of South Dakota, the soldiers soon had a nice break from their grueling journey. On July 3, they arrived in Crawford, Nebraska, where "the Corps was given a hearty welcome." The town was in a merry mood as residents were beginning their Fourth of July celebration. Quickly falling into a double-line formation, the Bicycle Corps pedaled down Crawford's main street "at a lively gait" while a band played and the crowd cheered. The next day, the men rode to Alliance, Nebraska, where they celebrated the holiday with a special feast. At the same time, they were also celebrating their 1,000-mile mark—they were more than halfway to St. Louis!

Unfortunately, the going got tough again as the corps pedaled on through Nebraska. Temperatures sometimes reached 110 degrees, but there was precious little water to be found. While their faces were soaked with sweat, their mouths were gritty and bone dry. The metal bicycles

In this article from the Daily Missoulian, *Edward Boos describes the corps' welcome in Crawford, Nebraska, on the Fourth of July.* —Courtesy Montana Historical Society Research Center, Library Collections, Helena, MT

got so hot that it became difficult even to hold onto the handlebars. On several occasions some of the men, including Lt. Moss himself, got so ill from drinking alkaline water that they were left behind to recover, later taking a train to catch up.

On July 16, the expedition reached the Missouri River, which marked the border between Nebraska and Missouri. They took a ferry across the river and stepped off—at last—onto Missouri soil. At this milestone, their spirits soared, knowing they would soon be arriving at their final destination.

St. Louis, Here We Come!

EDWARD BOOS, THE JOURNALIST WHO had been riding with the Bicycle Corps the whole way, had been sending regular reports back to the *Daily Missoulian*. Many of his articles were picked up by newspapers across the nation. By the time the men reached Missouri, their story was well known, and the public began to follow the progress of "Uncle Sam's Riders" with increasing excitement.

The crowds of people coming out to see the soldiers as they moved through Missouri became larger and larger. On July 24, as the corps neared St. Louis, a group of nearly 1,000 cyclists rode out to meet them and lead them into town. Thousands had gathered in the city's Forest Park to welcome the soldiers, greeting them with "hearty cheers."

The 1,900-mile expedition officially ended at the Cottage restaurant in Forest Park, where Lt. Moss gave his last order of the trip: "You will now rest wheels and fall in for mess." The men sat down to a delicious supper of juicy steak, fresh tomatoes, and buttered bread. The *St. Louis Star* called the corps' journey "the most marvelous cycling trip in the history of the wheel."

The entire trip had taken forty days, thirty-four of them actually spent traveling and six spent resting. Lt. Moss sent a letter to the War Department asking that the corps be allowed to continue on to St. Paul, Minnesota, to further test the bicycles. His request was denied, and the soldiers were ordered to return to Missoula by train. After resting in St. Louis for a week, the triumphant Bicycle Corps started their trip home, arriving back at Fort Missoula on August 19, 1897.

The Cottage restaurant in Forest Park, St. Louis, circa 1895
—Courtesy Missouri History Museum

Upon the corps' return from St. Louis, the lieutenant made numerous statements to the press, including a lengthy description in the *Los Angeles Times*, but his official report was his only detailed record of the expedition. In it, Lt. Moss praised his men for the "spirit, plunk and fine soldierly qualities they displayed" and noted that the journey had "tested to the utmost not only their physical endurance but their moral courage and disposition." It is for these qualities that history remembers them.

9. The End of the Experiment
Success or Failure?

AFTER THE BICYCLE CORPS returned from St. Louis, Lt. Moss, in commentary published in the *Army and Navy Journal*, declared the experiment an unqualified success:

The trip has proven beyond [a doubt] my contention that the bicycle has a place in modern warfare. In every kind of weather, over all sorts of roads, we averaged fifty miles a day. At the end of the journey we are all in good physical condition. Seventeen tires and half a dozen frames is the sum of our damage. The practical result of the trip shows that an Army Bicycle Corps can travel twice as fast as cavalry or infantry under any condition, and at one third the cost and effort.

Although Moss's overall assessment was strongly positive, he did note several problems that would have to be addressed for future trips. Among his suggestions for improvement were these: 1) rations should be increased; 2) shock absorbers should be added to the handlebars of the bicycles; 3) puncture-proof tires would be helpful; 4) to ease strain and avoid needless injury, the men should not carry their rifles on their backs.

While Moss was enthusiastic about the bicycle's potential for military use, he was not suggesting that cyclists could totally replace the cavalry. He believed that the Bicycle Corps would be very effective as messengers and scouts for both cavalry and infantry, and that such a unit would be useful in situations that required speed, efficiency, and stealth.

In spite of the good reasons to establish a permanent Bicycle Corps, the U.S. Army would not pursue the idea any further. The limitations of the bicycle in bad weather and over rough terrain may have dampened the military's motivation to invest in the equipment and training needed. In February 1898, Lt. Moss asked permission to make another bike trip, this time from Fort Missoula to San Francisco, California. Col. Burt supported the proposal as a goodwill tour that would continue the positive race relationships seen along the way on the trip to St. Louis:

> It is well known that there is a prejudice against the colored man. . . . It is a wise policy to educate the people to become familiar with the colored man as a soldier. . . . The expedition proposed by Lt. Moss would be a fine educator. The one he made last year to St. Louis had a very happy effect. The men by their behavior won the respect of everybody.

The War Department denied the request.

Col. Andrew Burt, date unknown —Courtesy Robert Snow

Off to War

EVEN HAD MOSS'S TRIP been approved, however, it probably would have been canceled because of a serious new development: war. Tensions had been brewing between the United States and Spain for several years when, on February 15, 1898, the U.S. battleship *Maine* exploded in the harbor at Havana, Cuba. The public assumed it had been a deliberate attack by the Spanish, and the call to war rang out.

The 25th Infantry was one of the first units ordered to Cuba to respond to the hostilities that would soon become the Spanish-American War. On April 10, 1898, which happened to be Easter Sunday, the 25th Infantry left Fort Missoula for training camps in Georgia and Florida. That morning, the citizens of Missoula lined the streets to bid the Buffalo Soldiers good-bye as they marched off to war. The *Daily Missoulian* reported:

The citizens of Missoula turned out en masse to see the boys off. The line of march was lined with our own citizens and many country folks who had come miles to see the troops depart. As the boys in blue passed through the streets with band playing and colors gaily flying, most likely for the last time in this city, they never presented a prettier picture. . . .

Col. Burt was much moved by the outpouring of support:

In all my 36 years of service in the army I have never seen a more popular turnout to bid troops farewell . . . than was accorded us by the people of Missoula this morning. It made me feel proud and I wish to express . . . my thanks and hearty appreciation to the kind people of Missoula for the demonstration.

The 25th Infantry went on to serve honorably in Cuba, especially during the Battle of El Caney. Two other regiments of Buffalo Soldiers, the 9th and 10th Cavalry, were particularly praised for their instrumental role in future president Theodore Roosevelt's victory at San Juan Hill, a major battle in the Spanish-American War.

A crowd of Missoula residents gathers downtown to say farewell to the 25th Infantry as they leave to fight in the Spanish-American War in Cuba, 1898. —Courtesy Archives & Special Collections, Mansfield Library, University of Montana (76-0200)

The regiment shown in this 1899 photograph is unknown, but many Buffalo Soldiers, including the 25th Infantry, served in the Spanish-American War. —Courtesy Library of Congress

After the war, the various companies of the 25th Infantry were split up and assigned to different posts. Many of these soldiers were sent to the Philippines in 1899 to put down a rebellion there, again serving admirably. But racial bigotry in America was still intense, and the men were often treated badly by their own countrymen, especially in the South. One battalion of the 25th would eventually be sent to Texas, where an unjust fate awaited them.

10. Legacy

Honoring the Bicycle Corps

ALTHOUGH the U.S. Army conducted several more experiments with bicycles, it never established a permanent Bicycle Corps. After the Spanish-American War ended, Lt. Moss drew up a proposal to have 100 soldiers on bicycles ride through Havana, Cuba, to prevent riots, but his plan was never implemented. Nevertheless, the army did employ bicycles during World Wars I and II as supplementary transportation.

James Moss served in the army until 1922, and he was eventually promoted to the rank of colonel. After accompanying the 25th Infantry to Cuba, he served with another black regiment, the 24th Infantry, in the Philippines. During World War I, he commanded the 367th Infantry, also a mostly African American unit. All of his commands earned praise and honors. Later, in addition to numerous instructional manuals for the military, Moss wrote books on the history of the U.S. flag and spearheaded the move to make Flag Day (June 14) an official holiday, which happened in 1916. James A. Moss died in 1941 in a car accident in New York City; he was buried at Arlington National Cemetery.

The Fate of the 25th Infantry

WHAT BECAME OF THE ENLISTED MEN of the 25th Infantry Bicycle Corps? According to military records, Eugene Jones was wounded while in Cuba during the Spanish-American War, and Elwood Forman died in the Philippines in 1901. Dalbert Green served in the army for twenty-five years and retired in 1916. Sgt. William Haynes was again stationed at Fort Missoula for a time. William Brown retired to California.

After the Philippines conflict, most of the remaining members of the 25th were sent to Fort Niobrara in Nebraska. In 1906 the 1st Battalion was transferred to Fort Brown in Brownsville, Texas, where the soldiers became caught up in a notorious incident known as the "Brownsville Affair."

The racist residents of Brownsville had made it known that they did not want the Buffalo Soldiers in their community, but the army sent them anyway. Among the former Bicycle Corps riders stationed at Fort Brown at the time were Pvt. John Cook and 1st Sgt. Mingo Sanders. Sanders was nearing retirement after twenty-five years of military service and had an outstanding record. In the middle of the night on August 13, 1906, a shooting by unidentified assailants occurred for unknown reasons. A white civilian was shot dead in the incident and another was wounded. The crime was linked to the soldiers of the 25th Infantry.

When none of the men admitted guilt, it was assumed that they were all covering up for one another. No hearing was held and none of the soldiers were brought to trial. Instead, the entire battalion, 167 men, was discharged without honor by executive order from the president. Ironically, that president was Theodore Roosevelt, whose neck had been saved by Buffalo Soldiers in Cuba.

The discharge without honor meant that the soldiers were denied their pensions, were ineligible for reenlistment, and could not hold any federal job. A reexamination of the case sixty-six years later reversed the charges, and Congress granted the men of the 1st Battalion honorable discharges on September 28, 1972, long after most of them had died. In fact, only one soldier, eighty-six-year-old Dorrie Willis, lived to see his vindication.

Protecting Parks, Fighting Fires

IN THE LATE 1800s and early 1900s, before the introduction of federal park rangers, the 25th Infantry and other units of Buffalo Soldiers patrolled the national parks of Montana, Wyoming, California, and elsewhere. It is unknown whether any of the members of the Bicycle Corps served in this capacity, but some of the other men of the 25th Infantry did.

The earliest Buffalo Soldiers in Glacier National Park, for example, were literally trailblazers who explored, mapped, and carved trails in the park's wild regions. For two decades, soldiers of the 25th Infantry and other units built roads, fought fires, maintained order at nearby mining camps, and protected federal lands from illegal grazing, logging, and poaching in Glacier, Yellowstone, Yosemite, and other parks.

In the summer of 1910, a series of ferocious wildfires broke out in Montana and Idaho. Among those called in to help fight

This 1911 painting, Putting out the Campfire *by Frederick Maladore Spiegle, shows men fighting the Great Fire of 1910. It appeared in a 1915 pamphlet published by the Western Forestry and Conservation Association and many years later, on a commemorative poster. The 25th Infantry were among the troops sent to help control the flames.* —Courtesy Archives & Special Collections, Mansfield Library, University of Montana (Northern Montana Forestry Association Records, Mss 034)

the flames were the men of the 25th Infantry, including two companies from Fort Missoula. One company of the 25th, led by Lt. W. S. Mapes, fought severe fires in Glacier National Park. In a letter to the Secretary of the Interior, the park superintendent applauded the company's dedication and courage:

> *I doubt if I can say enough in praise of Lt. Mapes and his negro troops. The work performed by them could not be improved upon by any class of men. To their lot fell the worst fire in the park and they went at its extinguishment with snap and energy, built roads and trail and miles and miles of fire guard trenches without the least sign of discontent. I believe that it is only fair . . . that you call the War Department's attention to the splendid work performed by them, as they certainly deserve commendation.*

Montanans Remember the Corps

IN 1974 TWO PROFESSORS from the Black Studies Department at the University of Montana, Pferron Doss and Richard Smith, organized a trip to honor the accomplishments of the Bicycle Corps. Leaving Missoula on June 14, the seventy-seventh anniversary of the corps' departure, ten cyclists followed the soldiers' route from Missoula to St. Louis. On the paved streets and highways of the late twentieth century, the group worried more about traffic than terrain. In spite of their advantages of modern roads and equipment, however, they faced the same steep hills and bad weather. Doss noted that "It was not until we were pedaling down their shadows that we could fully appreciate what they endured."

Professor Pferron Doss at the University of Montana in 1974,
preparing for his trip to trace the cross-country route of the
Bicycle Corps —Courtesy Historical Museum at Fort Missoula

While a number of books and articles have been published
about the corps, this piece of history remains little known. In
2000, Montana PBS and the University of Montana produced
a documentary film titled *The Bicycle Corps: America's Black
Army on Wheels.* In addition, the Historical Museum at Fort
Missoula maintains an extensive collection of information,

photographs, and artifacts relating to the Bicycle Corps and other chapters of the fort's past. Remnants of the original post still stand, but the surrounding area is, of course, radically different. While a portion of the original grounds of Fort Missoula is now a historical museum complex, much of the remaining acreage is used for community recreation.

The noncommissioned officers' quarters, built in 1878, is one of the few original fort buildings that is still standing at Fort Missoula today. —Photo by Jay Kettering

The Long Road to Equality

THE BUFFALO SOLDIERS SERVED at a time when racial discrimination was very prevalent in America. Many of these soldiers joined the military hoping that if they served their country well, attitudes might change. African American military historian Edward Johnson noted in 1899 that the Buffalo Soldier "did his duty under the flag, whether that flag protected him or not."

It was not until after World War II that racial segregation officially ended in the U.S. military, when President Harry Truman signed Executive Order 9981, which mandated the integration of the armed forces, in 1948. And it was not until the Civil Rights Act of 1964 that racial discrimination was outlawed in the United States; this was followed by the Civil Rights Act of 1968, affirmative action, and other laws. One might argue that the positive example set by the Bicycle Corps helped "set the wheels in motion" for racial equality and social justice.

In 1992 Congress designated July 28, the anniversary of the creation of the original four black regiments, to be Buffalo Soldiers Day. The same week, a fourteen-foot statue of a black frontier soldier was dedicated at Fort Leavenworth, Kansas. Although the soldier in the sculpture is posed on a horse, not a bicycle, it's a deserving tribute.

The next time you ride a bicycle, think of what "Uncle Sam's Riders" went through. You will probably agree that the Buffalo Soldiers of the Bicycle Corps were some of the greatest unsung pioneers of the American West.

The Buffalo Soldier Monument at Fort Leavenworth
—Courtesy Frontier Army Museum, Fort Leavenworth, KS

Acknowledgments

I WANT TO EXPRESS MY APPRECIATION to the many people who assisted me in the development of this book. It is rewarding to know that bicycle history is kept alive by the various bicycle museums throughout the country. Thank you especially to the Houston Bicycle Museum and the Bicycle Museum of America for their help. When I visited Missoula, the people at the Historical Museum at Fort Missoula generously opened their files about the Bicycle Corps to me, and the archivists at the Mansfield Library, University of Montana, were extremely helpful in sharing authentic photographs of the city and the Buffalo Soldiers.

This book would not be as informative and organized without the skills of Gwen McKenna, editor extraordinaire. Thank you for your patience as I juggled a full-time university teaching load with book revisions and photograph gathering.

My sister, Carol Pervi, read an early version of this manuscript and offered useful clarifying suggestions. I deeply appreciate that Dr. Armin R. Schulz of California State University, Stanislaus, an expert in juvenile literature, provided a critical review of the manuscript before his untimely passing. He was a dear friend whom I miss greatly. My son, Bryan, was my fellow researcher in Missoula. I appreciate the many things he does to support all my literary efforts.

Bibliography

Bailey, Linda C. *Fort Missoula's Military Cyclists: The Story of the 25th U.S. Infantry Bicycle Corps.* Missoula, Mont.: Friends of the Historical Museum at Fort Missoula, 1997.

Boos, Edward H. Dispatches to *Daily Missoulian*, June 14, 1897–July 29, 1897.

Carroll, John M., ed. *The Black Military Experience in the American West.* New York: Liveright Publishing, 1971.

David, Jay, and Elaine Crane, eds. *The Black Soldier: From the American Revolution to Vietnam.* New York: William Morrow, 1971.

Fitzpatrick, Jim. *The Bicycle in Wartime: An Illustrated History.* Washington, D.C.: Brassey's, 1998.

Fletcher, Marvin E. *The Black Soldier and Officer in the United States Army 1891–1917.* Columbia: University of Missouri Press, 1974.

_____. "The Black Bicycle Corps." In *A Question of Manhood: A Reader in U.S. Black Men's History and Masculinity.* Vol. 2. Edited by Earnestine Jenkins and Darlene Clark Hine. Bloomington: Indiana University Press, 2001.

Lanning, Michael Lee. *The African-American Soldier: From Crispus Attucks to Colin Powell.* New York: Citadel Press, 1999.

Leckie, William H. *The Buffalo Soldiers: A Narrative of the Negro Cavalry in the West.* Norman: University of Oklahoma Press, 1967.

Nankivell, John H., ed. *The History of the Twenty-Fifth Regiment, United States Infantry, 1869–1926.* Fort Collins, Colo.: Old Army Press, 1972.

Moss, James A. "Military Cycling in the Rocky Mountains." In *Spalding's Athletic Library.* New York: American Sports Publishing Company, 1897.

Sorensen, George Niels. *Iron Riders: Story of the 1890s Fort Missoula Buffalo Soldiers Bicycle Corps.* Missoula, Mont.: Pictorial Histories Publishing, 2000.

Children's/Young Adult

Cox, Clinton. *The Forgotten Heroes: The Story of the Buffalo Soldiers.* New York: Scholastic, 1996.

Katz, William Loren. *Black People Who Made the Old West.* New York: Thomas Y. Crowell, 1977.

Stovall, Taressa. *The Buffalo Soldiers.* Philadelphia, Pa.: Chelsea House Publishers, 1997.

Watson, Toni A. "The Great Bicycle Experiment." *Cobblestone,* February 1995.

Online Sources

Higgins, Mike. "The 25th Infantry Bicycle Corps." http://www
.bicyclecorps.blogspot.com/.

Historical Museum at Fort Missoula. "Black Bicycle Corps."
http://www.fortmissoulamuseum.org/blackbicyclecorps
.php.

Hosler, Lt. Col. Roderick A. "Hell on Two Wheels: The 25th
Infantry Bicycle Corps." http://armyhistoryjournal
.com/?p=396.

"U.S. Army's 25th Infantry Bicycle Corps: Wheels of War." Origi-
nally published in *American History* magazine. http://
www.historynet.com/us-armys-25th-infantry-bicycle
-corps-wheels-of-war.htm.

Index of Illustrations

Index

About the Author

Kay Moore was born and raised in Maryland, where she explored her grandparents' attic and discovered a Union soldier's drum from the Civil War, and her love for history was born. After ten years as a classroom teacher, she attended graduate school at the University of the Pacific and received her doctorate in education. Currently a professor in the Teacher Education Department at California State University in Sacramento, Kay is the author of several children's nonfiction books, including *If You Lived at the Time of the Civil War* (Scholastic, 1994), as well as professional guides for teachers. She lives in Placerville, California, not far from the site of the 1849 gold discovery that prompted the great California Gold Rush.